SCHOOL OF
TRUE WORSHIP
AND
EFFECTUAL FERVENT
PRAYER MANUAL

Written By
DR. DORN J. B. WALKER

Print ISBN: 978-1-66780-878-9
eBook ISBN: 978-1-66780-879-6

"THE MATERIAL CONTAINED IN THIS MANUAL IS THE EXPRESSED

BELIEF OF WALLS OF SALVATION CHURCH MINISTRIES, INC. AND IS ENCOURAGED AS A GUIDELINE FOR GODLY, REVERENTIAL WORSHIP AND EFFECTUAL FERVENT PRAYER."

Apostle John Y. Walker, Jr.
Dr. Dorn J.B. Walker

The scriptures are taken from the KING JAMES VERSION (KJV) public domain and the NEW KING JAMES VERSION (NKJV). The NEW KING JAMES VERSION®. Copyright© 1982 by Thomas Nelson, Inc. Used by permission. All rights reserved.

Some scriptures are also taken from the Amplified Bible, Classic Edition (AMPC). The Amplified® Bible, Copyright © 1954, 1958, 1962, 1964, 1965, 1987 by The Lockman Foundation Used by permission." (www.Lockman.org)

Take note that we have not capitalized the names such as "satan" and other related demonic names. We choose to not highlight or acknowledge him and his followers. Therefore, we have ignored and violated grammatical rules to make our point. Occasionally, we have emphasized, underlined, and highlighted certain scripture references for amplification.

No reproduction of this material is permitted without expressed written permission. For questions, comments, conference, and other instructional booking for your group, please contact Walls of Salvation Church Ministries, Inc. via one of the following methods:

P.O. BOX 19082
PENSACOLA, FLORIDA 32523
woscministries@bellsouth.net
Facebook: **Pastor John Walker Jr.**
Phone: **850-457-3487**
www.wallsofsalvation.global

DEDICATION AND ACKNOWLEDGMENTS

I dedicate this curriculum book to my first pastors, the late Dr. Charles Phillips, and his lovely widow, Dr. Cheryl Phillips. Their ministry introduced me to the importance of having a lifestyle of worship and fervent prayer. It is my belief that these two principles are critical and foundational to the health and maturity of every believer's walk with Christ. I have been so blessed to have begun my walk with Christ under the mentorship of these great leaders.

To my husband and current pastor, Apostle John Walker, Jr., I love you and want to thank you for providing me the opportunity for over 10 years to freely teach and demonstrate —"The School of True Worship and Effectual Fervent Prayer" at the Church you founded. I am grateful that you allowed the vision of this curriculum to merge with and enhance the vision God gave you for the Walls of Salvation Church Ministries.

Lastly, but most importantly, I thank you Holy Spirit for truly teaching me all things (John 14:26). Spirit of Truth, You have forever set the foundation of my walk with Father God. I desire to stay connected to the True Vine. This intimacy I have found in You can never be replaced by anyone or by anything in this world. Thank you, Jesus, for making my intimate walk with God possible through Your atoning sacrifice. Thank you, God, for resurrecting Jesus from the dead and allowing me to receive and become empowered by the same Spirit that raised up Jesus. I am so grateful to be free to live the abundant life of an unbroken fellowship with Father God through Your precious Holy Spirit.

TOPIC CONTENTS

FOREWORD

Through this curriculum book, you will become a student of true worship and learn how to become an effective intercessor who ushers heaven to earth as Elder Dorn escorts you on a journey that will transform your worship and prayer life. She is truly an authentic gift to others from the Body of Christ who displays God's presence and power to the nations of the world. She has a fire and passion that distinguishes her from other giftings. This book will challenge leaders, laypersons, and members of the Body of Christ to become true worshipers and effectual fervent prayer warriors. It will equip you with essential tools necessary to "Fight the Good Fight" of Faith and "Wage Successful Warfare" against the forces of darkness.

One of my favorite character traits about Elder Dorn is that she does not half do a task or project. When she completes a project, she turns over every stone with excellence. This book will go into some deep spiritual matters that will guide the new believer, seasoned saint, or the experienced intercessor. It contains God's impartation and ammunition downloaded from Heaven. Open your heart and get ready to put the principles cited in this book into operation. They will assist you in your personal walk and corporate fellowship in the Body of Christ.

Elder Dorn has trained ambassadors at the Walls of Salvation Church Ministries and at other churches with the trues contained in this book for over 10 years. I am so immensely proud of my wife, the author, who has opened the classroom of her encounters with God so that others may benefit from her journey. I trust that at the end of this book, you will encounter a higher dimension of God and discover your violent spiritual man that wages war against the devil while declaring total victory.

Apostle John Walker, Jr.
Founding Pastor, Walls of Salvation Church Ministries, Inc.
Pensacola, Florida
wallsofsalvation.global

INTRODUCTION

This curriculum book is designed to be used as a practical tool to enhance your own spiritual growth, as you mature and develop a greater intimate relationship with Jesus Christ. It can also be used as an instructional manual in your church, or in small or large group studies with like-minded believers who desire deeper fellowship with God in an empowering corporate setting. Whether you are a student or a teacher of this "True Worship and Effectual Fervent Prayer" manual and curriculum book, you will discover profound insights into a rewarding, victorious, abundant life led by God's precious Holy Spirit. The Word of God tells us in Romans 8:14, *"for as many as are led by the Spirit of God, these are sons of God."* The exciting news is that as sons (and daughters) of God, we are also heirs and joint heirs with Jesus Christ in God's Kingdom. Let us embrace God's Word that declares we are more than conquerors. We have kingdom dominion authority!

Since I began my walk with the Lord Jesus Christ in 1987, I have found that one of the most valuable aspects of my walk with God is to understand, embrace, and practice the essence of "True Worship". Also, it is critical that we develop a consistent life of "Effectual Fervent Prayer" while living in this world of increasing darkness. I believe that these two topics are inseparable. As a True Worshiper and as a prayer warrior and intercessor, God shows Himself mightily through us and use our lives as a shining beacon of light in a lost and dying world. In this manual, one can also discover that we are not just living a life on the defense when issues arise, but we are also offensive, victorious warriors who place the enemy under our feet as we boldly declare that he is illegally trespassing. No matter what difficulty may come our way, we make a conscious decision to press forward and advance the Kingdom of God in the earth.

I pray that after you read and study this curriculum book, you will likewise make a similar discovery that propels you into a deeper fellowship and relationship with our Lord and Savior Jesus Christ. Jesus Christ opened the way for us to enter the holy of holies in the presence of Abba Father. This is the place where we daily fellowship with God our Maker and Creator through His precious Holy Spirit. God desires that we walk in victory and live life and have life more abundantly.

I believe that each student should also become a teacher after wisdom has been fully imparted. Therefore, my prayer is that you also would share and pass on this valuable information to other believers. May God's precious Holy Spirit breathe through each page and bring life to your walk, as you seek a more intimate fellowship with God and become a bold representative of God's Kingdom in the earth!

TRUE

WORSHIP

TRUE WORSHIP

GOAL

The goal of this section is to bring the reader into an understanding of "True Worship." This section will challenge the reader to look deeper into God's original intent for worship and to also understand that God is still seeking worshipers to represent Him in the earth.

Our God, Yahweh (one of the Hebrew names for God), is our relational God who desires to commune with us daily. If you are in search of a closer intimate relationship with God or you have been trying to lead others into an understanding of what it means to have a relationship with God, the material in this section will reward and equip you with the valuable and essential information you are seeking. It will provide you with practical knowledge of "True Worship."

WHAT YOU WILL NEED TO GET STARTED

To receive the greatest benefit from this section, I suggest the following:

a. An enthusiastic desire for fellowship with your Creator,

b. The Word of God in any format that is easily accessible,

c. A quiet space that is free of distractions,

d. An honest, willing, and teachable heart,

e. It is recommended that you use a journal to track your spiritual growth and for planning your times of fellowship with God. A journal is also important for writing down your visions, plans, and purposes of God that you may receive from God during your time of "True Worship." NOW ENJOY AND ALLOW YOURSELF TO BECOME ADDICTED TO HIS PRESENCE

TRUE WORSHIP DEFINED

John 4:23-24 say: "But the hour is coming, and now is, when the true worshipers will worship the Father in spirit and in truth; for the Father is seeking such to worship Him. God is Spirit, and those who worship Him must worship Him in spirit and in truth." (NKJV)

Worship is a direct manifestation of our personal intimate relationship and fellowship with God. Today, people worship many things. However, as believers in God's Kingdom, we must direct our worship to the Almighty God, maker of Heaven and Earth to remain in a healthy relationship and keep unbroken fellowship with Him. Our God is a Jealous God, and He will have no other gods before Him (See Exodus 20:5, Exodus 34:14). In fact, one of God's names is JEALOUS. His Hebrew name El-Kanna implies that not only is He Jealous about His creation, but HIS name is JEALOUS (See Deuteronomy 4:24, Deuteronomy 5:9, Deuteronomy 6:15, Joshua 24:19, and Nahum 1:2). God is enthusiastic and serious about His creation, and He wants to fellowship with us.

When we worship God, He becomes the center of our attention and focus on life. **Take a Selah moment (pause and calmly think about it). What do we worship?** We worship:

(1) Whatever we are committed and devoted to--the object of our constant focus,

(2) Whatever we live for and would die for and whatever we can never live without, and

(3) Whatever we love with all our heart, soul, mind, and strength and are willing to sacrifice our entire life for—including our time, alms, gifts, the things we own, including our money.

Many believers play and enjoy music. Some dance and even sing with music and often refer to these acts as worship. However, worship is not just about what we do with music. First, we must have a heart and passion to draw closer to God so that we will understand the importance of taking time out for intimate fellowship and positioning ourselves with God.

James 4:8 (NKJV) tells us to "Draw near to God and He will draw near to you."

God wants to fellowship with us. He is jealous over his creation and wants to be close to us. Do you have a passion and a burning desire to commune daily with the Almighty God? He is patiently waiting to fellowship with you. He wants "true worship."

A CLOSER LOOK AT TRUE WORSHIP

Let us take a closer look at what the Bible says about "True Worship." In John 4:23, the word "true" is the Greek word "alethinos (pronounced al-ay-thee-nos). It is used to describe God's worshipers. In this scripture, true is used as an adjective and signifies being "real," "ideal," and "genuine". Therefore, God's worshipers are expected to be real, ideal, and genuine. The Bible uses the same Greek word to describe God in the following scriptures:

> *John 7:28 states: "Then cried Jesus in the temple as he taught, saying, Ye both know me, and ye know whence I am: and I am not come of myself, but he that sent me is true, whom ye know not." (KJV)*

> **John 17: 3 also uses this Greek word to describe God:**

> *"And this is eternal life: [it means] to know (to perceive, recognize, become acquainted with, and understand) You, the only true and real God, and [likewise] to know Him, Jesus [as the]*

Christ (the anointed One, the Messiah), Whom You have sent."
(Amplified)

I Thessalonians 1:9 says: "For they themselves volunteer testi-
mony concerning us, telling what an entrance we had among you,
and how you turned to God from [your] idols to serve a God Who
is alive and true and genuine." (Amplified)

Lastly, Revelation 6: 10 says: "And they cried with a loud voice,
saying, how long, O Lord, holy and true, dost thou not judge and
avenge our blood on them that dwell on the earth?" (KJV)

God is saying to us that He fulfills the meaning of His name. He is the
<u>True</u> God in distinction from all other false gods. He is also saying that
He is <u>true</u> to His utterances—He cannot lie. This can be summarized to
say: "God says what He means, and He means what He says." Also, He is
who He is--One with Himself. God is Holy.

This Greek word for "True" (Alethinos) is also found in I John 5:20 where
it speaks of the purpose of Jesus Christ. This scripture says: *"And we know*
that the Son of God is come, and hath given us an understanding, that
we may know Him Who is true, and we are in Him Who is true, even
in His Son Jesus Christ. This is the true God, and eternal life." (KJV)

Alethinos (True) defines the relationship of the conception to the thing
to which it corresponds. In other words—the one who is made under-
stands the One by whom he is made. By design, he responds out of this
same character to his Creator in a true, real, ideal, and genuine form of
worship. This is all he knows, and desires. He lives, moves, and has his
very being in God. He deliberately, intentionally, and unapologetically
worships God from the core of his being. He knows that to "Worship God
we live, and we live to Worship God." God created us to worship Him
and Him alone! AMEN. Just as God says be ye holy as I am holy---He
is equally saying to us - "worship Me and serve Me truly because I am

True." Furthermore, God is saying that if we are in Him, we know Him who is True—and we will also be true—Amen.

HOW DOES THE BIBLE DESCRIBE "WORSHIP"?

The English word "Worship" is often limited to our frame of reference (What we perceive this word to mean based on our experiences but not necessarily the fullness of what it means). However, the original Hebrew (Old Testament words of the Bible were originally written in the Hebrew language) and Greek (New Testament words of the Bible were originally written in the Greek language) words give us a deeper and clearer understanding of this word "Worship." The Bible clearly describes the various actions of adoration toward God with some key words. Let's look at a few of these words.

The Hebrew word Shachah (pronounced Shaw-khaw) and the Greek word Proskaneo (pronounced pros-Koo-neh-o) are used most often in the Bible to describe worship. Therefore, we will begin defining "Worship" with these two words.

SHACHAH means to depress (to decrease, lower or to slow down). For example, it means prostrate (facedown, level to the ground, powerless, horizontal) in homage to God. It means to bow, bow down, obeisance (gesture of respect or reverence –For example, bend, bob – acknowledge), reverence, fall down, stoop, crouch) SHACHAH is an act of bowing down in homage by an inferior before a superior ruler (the Sovereign God). The Bible first mentions Shachah in Genesis 22:5.

PROSKUNEO is derived from the Greek word: "pros" which means toward or forward, by the side of, near to (the destination of the relation—for which it is affirmed or predicated), according to, because of, within. PROSKUNEO means to make obeisance, do reverence to. Pros means toward and KUNEO means to kiss. It is an act of homage

or reverence to God. To crouch; to prostrate oneself; to adore. In the New Testament, Proskuneo is first mentioned in Matthew 2:2.

<u>Other words for worship include:</u>

LATREUO (pronounced lat-ryoo-o) means to minister to God, render, serve, to work for, of service to God (one walking in purpose and destiny – walking in our earthly calling and assignment). As used in <u>Philippians 3:3</u>, Paul describes the believers' service as an act of spiritual obedience. Paul reminds us not to judge a person's spirituality based on their fulfillment of duties, works or activities. We can never satisfy God by doing our own works. We merely serve God and respond to Him as He speaks to our hearts.

SEBOMAI (pronounced seb-om-ahee) means to feel awe, revere, adore, devout. This word is used in Acts 18:13 describing Paul's preaching of the Gospel by the Jews who opposed him.

<u>Take a Selah moment.</u>

Have you ever worshiped God in any of the ways and postures described in the aforementioned Hebrew and Greek words? Take time out now to ask the Holy Spirit to further expound the meanings of these words that define "Worship."

Now allow your understanding of the words "True" and "Worship" to deepen. Daily practice your time alone with God as defined in the Bible and flow into "True Worship."

REPRESENTING THE EKKLESIA

Worship is a vital part of the Ekklesia (This Greek word is commonly used to identify the assembly of those called out of darkness by God into His marvelous light—to shine ever so brightly in a dark and often dimly lit world). The Ekklesia is the <u>Church and God is looking for us to light up the world. We must pierce every darkness and keep the world "lit."</u>

Can God identify you by your Worship? This is your connection with Him to hear His voice and to receive instructions through your time with Him. God does not desire our traditions, cultures, religious acts and the types of buildings or edifices in which we gather. God is still seeking True Worshipers. He is looking for those who will worship Him in spirit and truth. Therefore, we must humble ourselves and understand that Religion, Culture, good works, and the quantity of our material possessions do not identify God's Church or His Body of Believers. God is looking for True Worshipers. True Worshipers are not moved by circumstances or by their surroundings – but only by God's precious Holy Spirit.

HOW IMPORTANT IS OUR WORSHIP?

Everything God made has an ideal environment—and a place where it functions best. For example, Genesis Chapter 1 tells us that before God made the Sun, the Moon and stars, God called forth the light and separated it from the darkness calling the light day and the darkness night. Then God made a firmament–the sky. Finally, He set the lights in the sky. Also, before God spoke the plants and animals into being, He gathered the waters together so that the dry ground would appear (the land) and the waters He called the seas. Then God commanded the seas to bring forth the sea creatures and to the land He commanded it to bring forth vegetation, plants, trees, cattle, and all living creatures. We clearly see here that every part of God's creation has its perfect place and ideal environment for proper functioning.

Likewise, before God created and made man, God decided how He would make Man and He also decided on the ideal environment for Man. God decided on man's specific dwelling–where He would place His creation. **Genesis 1:26-27 and Chapter 2:8 (NKJV) tell us the foundation of Man's Worship which is the dwelling place that God created for**

him. When God planned that man would be made in His image and in His likeness **(John 4:24 tells us that God is a Spirit),** God also planned that man's environment or dwelling would be in Eden (the garden of the Lord, God. This is referenced in Isaiah 51:3 and Ezekiel 28:13). Eden was the place where God's presence touched the earth. God planted His presence in the earth and His presence became Man's perfect and ideal environment. Eden became man's perfect dwelling place for growth, maturity, spiritual health, and the place to have an unbroken fellowship with God. In these scriptures, we can clearly see that "worship" in an unbroken fellowship with God was the plan for humanity from the very beginning of time. (There were no songs, music, choirs, or services—God simply gave His presence as the first gift to man). One of God's names is the Hebrew word Ma'on which means (the Dwelling place). Hallelujah! God is truly Ma'on—our dwelling place! Our place of worship.

The worshiper must understand that after humanity sinned, he was separated from God—and separated from fellowship and worship with God. However, we must know that only through a belief in and accep-tance of Jesus Christ, can we return to "Eden"–the very presence or dwelling of God and back to living in that unbroken fellowship with God, our Creator. (Romans 10:13 (NKJV) tells *us "For whoever calls on the name of the Lord shall be saved."* Jesus Christ is our Lord and Savior and through the repentance of our sins and acceptance of Jesus in our hearts, we can return to the presence of God in unbroken fellowship with Him—The place where we function best.) (Also, see Romans 10:9 and 10).

The Worshiper knows that God is seeking those who understand that True Worship is critical for one's existence—the place where we properly thrive and function. Anything that functions outside of its ideal envi-ronment eventually malfunctions. However, since Jesus died to bring us back to fellowship with God, we do not have to malfunction. God made a way for our return to Him. Just as fish must stay in the water and plants in the ground to thrive and live—Worshipers must return to and stay in the presence of God to flourish, grow, and to maximize our true life. Worship is not based on a religion or a place but on the attitude and desire of our heart.

THE PROPHET AMOS SHOWED STRONG DEVOTION AND DEPENDENCY ON GOD

The Prophet Amos is an example of someone who entered the very emotions of God that propelled him into his life's purpose. Amos was a humble shepherd who worshiped God with his life. Through his worship experience, God gave him a vision of the future (Amos 1) and told him to take His message to Israel (Amos 7:15). Amos could have continued to work only in his secular vocation, but he chose to worship God with his entire life. He obeyed God and became a true man of God through his lifestyle of obedience. During the time of Amos, rich people oppressed the poor and made a mockery of religion. Fearlessly, Amos used his life to cry out for the poor. He was not complacent. No other concerns took the place of God in his life. He did not ignore those in need. (It is believed that Amos was wealthy since he was a herdsman and a skilled writer who read a lot of history. Nonetheless, he chose to worship God with his life).

Amos faithfully did what God called Him to do. He was able to do this by first hearing the voice of God through his reverence for God in worship. After he heard Gods' voice in worship, Amos moved in full obedience and lived a purpose filled life. It is important to note that during our time of worship, we become fully available to God, and He can use our lives to fulfill His will on the earth. *II Chronicles 16:9 says: "For the eyes of the Lord run to and fro throughout the whole earth, to show Himself strong on behalf of them whose heart is loyal to Him" (NKJV).* (Amos showed strong emotions toward God and worshiped Him with his entire being.) What a mighty witness of worship.

DAVID'S LIFE AS A WORSHIPER

DAVID WORSHIPED GOD DURING THE GOOD AND BAD TIMES

THE GOOD TIMES

God identified and chose David while he was just a worshiper tending his business in the fields. Then God took David through a tremendous life journey that changed his generation and the course of history forever. During this journey, David paused and wrote one of the most loved and treasured Psalms of all time—Psalm 23.

<u>Psalm 23 (KJV)</u>

> *"The Lord is my shepherd; I shall not want.*
>
> *2 He maketh me to lie down in green pastures: he leadeth me beside the still waters.*
>
> *3 He restoreth my soul: he leadeth me in the paths of righteousness for his name's sake.*
>
> *4 Yea, though I walk through the valley of the shadow of death, I will fear no evil: for thou art with me; thy rod and thy staff they comfort me.*
>
> *5 Thou preparest a table before me in the presence of mine enemies: thou anointest my head with oil; my cup runneth over.*
>
> *6 Surely goodness and mercy shall follow me all the days of my life: and I will dwell in the house of the Lord for ever."*

<u>Let us take a closer look at David's journey as a Chosen Worshiper.</u>

David wrote Psalm 23 after God took him on an amazing journey as a young shepherd boy minding his business, tending, and keeping sheep, and privately worshiping God in the fields. God took David to a place where he could have never imagined. Let us look at four phases of his journey as a worshiper.

Phase I – "Chosen and Anointed"

The History of Psalm 23 begins in I Samuel 16 verses 1-7 and verses 10-13. In these passages, we see God rejecting Saul (Israel's first King). Then, God tells Samuel (a Priest and Prophet) to stop mourning Saul's rejection and go choose and anoint a new King. Samuel obeyed God and traveled to the house of Jesse (David's Dad) where God sent him. Samuel observed seven of Jesse's sons who were well kept and distinguished. However, God told Samuel not to look at the outward appearance because the Lord looks at the heart. Therefore, Samuel could not choose any of Jesse's seven sons.

We often do not hear sermons about how David's family treated him prior to and during this visit by Samuel. Imagine your dad preparing to meet with a well-known and respected priest and prophet. This guest was the person who chose the first King of Israel. All your brothers were chosen to attend a sacrifice and parade before this important person in hopes that they would be chosen as the next King, but you were not chosen to attend. No one even considered you as a choice. They thought that you were not important at all to attend this meeting. Therefore, you were not invited. Then all your brothers displayed their best disposition in the hopes of being chosen by Samuel. Although your daddy thought you were too young or too simple to be presented and considered, God had other plans for you because you touched His heart—as a worshiper. You spent time with Him and moved Him as He moved your spirit. Verse 12 of I Samuel 16 tells us of Jesse's eighth son—David who was red faced (ruddy) but chosen and anointed as Israel's next King. Imagine what was going through David's mind. David was probably thinking–Wow God! I did not realize that I meant that much to You. This is too deep for me. You chose and anointed me?

Phase II – "Publicly Appointed"

Secondly, in I Samuel 16:15-17 and verse 19, the verses show us that after David was anointed King, an evil spirit entered Saul and Saul became depressed. Again, young David was sought out. This time, David was appointed as the skilled musician to comfort Saul and bring him deliverance. God brought David out of his secret time of worship in the fields to a place of public ministry. Think about it, David journeyed from the "Pasture" to minister in the "Palace"—playing music for the same King that he was soon to replace.

Phase III – "Empowered Giant Slayer"

Thirdly, as David was minding his business, Saul's army was about to go to war with the Philistines. Goliath the Philistine giant threatened Israel for 40 days. When David's dad asked him to take food for his three older brothers who were in the war with the Philistines, David found himself in a battle with the giant, Goliath. David successfully killed the giant who threatened his people for more than a month. We can conclude here that David's time in worship with God, strengthened, empowered, and taught him how to be strong in the Lord and in the power of His might. In this posture, David was not afraid of giants. He knew that His God was with him, and that God was a mighty deliverer. In I Samuel 17:45 and 46 (NKJV) David made this confident statement: ***"You come to me with a sword, with a spear, and with a javelin. But I come to you in the name of the Lord of hosts, the God of the armies of Israel, whom you have defied. This day the Lord will deliver you into my hand…"*** God empowered David in his daily worship encounters. David became a bold, courageous, confident giant slayer!

Phase IV – "Endowed with God's Favor"

Finally, I Samuel 18:2 tells us that after David defeated Goliath, Saul took David into the palace to live permanently with him. I Samuel chapter 18 continues to tell us that King Saul's son, Jonathan began to love David as his own soul. Then, Jonathan decided to give David his royal robe, his garments, his sword, his bow, and his girdle. Jonathan adorned David as if he were cloaking him to become the next heir of the throne. This is amazing and deeply symbolic of the favor that God endowed upon David's life. Jonathan, (Saul's son and rightful heir to the throne) suddenly decided to cloak David as if he knew that David was chosen by God to be the heir. This was the moment when David became astoundingly overwhelmed. David reflected on the four phases of his life's journey and began to declare Psalm 23. David declared:

"The Lord is my Shepherd; I shall not want"

He understood that as a worshiper, God controlled his life. Worshipers understand that we are as sheep in God's pasture, and we lack nothing but Him. Even when David's family rejected him, the Lord chose and anointed him.

"He maketh me to lie down in green pastures: He leadeth me besides the still waters"

David knew that God prospers us in everything we touch. He never wastes our gifts or talents. As David played his instrument in secret, God rewarded him publicly. Our gifts, consecrated and dedicated to God, will always make room for us, and bring us in the presence of great men. God has placed gifts and talents in all of us. These gifts are not for secret use but to glorify His name and to bring healing and deliverance to others. God gives us peace amid every storm and often uses the momentum of our storms to refresh others as God used David to refresh King Saul.

"He restoreth my soul"

David understood that during worship, God refreshes and heals our mind and bruised emotions. When David thought that he was least in his family, God chose him as number one. The first shall be the last and the last shall be the first. Wait for God to complete you. When we are restored in Him, He will then introduce and present our lives publicly to the world to bring healing and restoration to others.

"He leadeth me in the paths of righteousness for His name's sake"

David understood that it is God who chooses us and not man. Man looks at the outward appearance, while God looks at the heart. God has a specific plan and purpose for our lives that will bring glory to His name.

"Yea, though I walk through the valley of the shadow of death, I will fear no evil: for thou art with me; thy rod and thy staff they comfort me"

David came to know God as his protector, deliverer, and comforter even in his valley moment as he faced Goliath. God kept David during this battle, and He will keep us as we face our giants. Our worship is a warship (worship becoming our strength in any battle) and God has called us and empowered us to slay giants!

"Thou preparest a table before me in the presence of my enemies: thou anointest my head with oil; my cup runneth over. Surely goodness and mercy shall follow me all the days of my life"

As a worshiper, David knew that God had an ultimate plan to make him heir of the throne. God's plan for David was publicly confirmed when Jonathan came in agreement with that plan. God's goodness and mercy continued to follow David throughout his life as he left the pasture and ended up in the palace where he would become King.

Worshipers, God has an ultimate plan for all of us. Worship Him intentionally and unapologetically. God is seeking you out. You are identified and chosen by your worship. Allow Him to take you on the most incredible journey of your life!

"And I will dwell in the house of the Lord forever, and ever Amen".

David understood that his success would always be dependent on his continuous worship and connection with God. God wants to take all of us on an amazing journey. But He needs to know the condition of our hearts—Will He be able to identify us and choose us by our sold-out life as a Worshiper? We are living in a serious time, and it is important that we get our hearts right before God and stay right so that God would be ready to identify us and send us on a mandate that can change the course of history.

After David's initial journey with God, he remained a man after God's own heart even in difficult and challenging situations. David continuously brought himself near to God and humbled himself even when he found himself outside of a right relationship with the Lord. Therefore, David can be described as a man who was not necessarily perfect but, he was "blameless" before God. Although he later sinned in his life, David did not park at any sinful address. Instead, he allowed God to restore Him by creating a clean heart and renewing a right spirit within him. David was able to give all his issues to God during his time of worship. Worship will clean us up and keep us transparent and blameless before God.

IN BAD TIMES, DAVID RAN TO GOD AND WORSHIPED HIM!

David wrote Psalm 27, after sin turned him away from God. Psalm 27 was written during a time when David and his people were destitute and in a desert wilderness (naturally and spiritually). David was now King, but he fled his throne with many of his people after his son Absalom tried to dethrone him and take his life. This account is found in II Samuel Chapters 11 through 18. Psalm 27 was written after David went through and was still going through much mourning and despair from the accounts of II Samuel chapters 11 – 18. (I recommend that you read and study these chapters for greater clarity.) A brief summary of these passages tell us that:

(1) David sinned with Bathsheba and in turn killed her husband, Uriah.

(2) Bathsheba became pregnant with David's child. The Child became ill and died.

(3) David's son Amnon raped his sister Tamar.

(4) Absalom, the other son, took vengeance and killed his brother Amnon.

(5) Absalom rebelled against his Father David to overthrow him from the throne. Then David gathered up His people and fled because he was afraid of Absalom and the evil that followed him.

This was the same King David that killed the great philistine giant Goliath. This was the same fearless worshiper. However, at this point in David's life, his heart was overwhelmed from mourning and despair which left him in a state of turmoil and weariness. His issues began to overtake him, and he lost sight of God ---Instead, David began to run from a mere man— His own son. II Samuel 17 states that David and His people became hungry, thirsty, and weary, in the wilderness. Not only was there a natural hunger, thirst, weariness, and loss of direction in the wilderness, but David also suffered from spiritual hunger and thirst for the righteousness of God, and he grew weary of toiling in his own strength which brought him to a spiritual destitute wilderness. However, II Samuel Chapter 17 shows that David later came to his senses, and he received both natural and spiritual provisions…this was about the time that David wrote Psalm 27.

David realized that his confidence was found only as he solely desired to run and return to his first love. This is the dwelling place of God. He then resubmitted his life fully to God.

In Psalm 27 (See the Amplified Bible), David stated that he desired and sought after one thing…To dwell in the house (not the physical church walls—but the very presence of God) of the Lord all the days of his life to behold the beauty of the Lord (the sweet attractiveness and presence of God) and to inquire in His temple. We are to remember that only the Holy Spirit can draw man to Christ. Leaders must have an intimate relationship with God to stay in right standing with God. We must become "Seeker Magnetic." This means, as we seek the very presence of God (the face of God), we will become magnetized by the Holy Spirit. Also, the power of God will flow through and from us like a consuming fire drawing others to Christ.

When we show no dependency on God or when we do not sense a hunger for God, our flesh is often controlling us. When this occurs, we must fast the things of the flesh to bring the flesh into subjection to the Holy Spirit and into a place of humility. (Fasting feeds our hunger for God. We deny the carnal and feed the spiritual.) Fasting from food is the most usual form of fasting. However, in our modern world filled with so many distractions, it is wise to temporally give up other carnal desires during a fast such as TV, social media, and other activities that may be hindering our fellowship with God.

IDOLATRY AND ADULTERY BEFORE GOD

What is Idolatry or adultery before God? Idolatry or adultery can be defined as blind or excessive adoration or love toward anything or anyone other than God. To idolize is to regard with unquestioning or excessive admiration or devotion. God's Word is clear concerning Idolatry. The Bible states that we are to have no other gods before Him, and that we are to try every spirit to see if it is from God—we shall know every spirit by the fruit it bears. But how many people are ignorant to the Idolatry that is raging rampant throughout the Body of Christ!

The Bible tells us that every believer's daily confidence is found only in the power of God and not in the wisdom of man or in any earthly carnal desire (I Corinthians 2:5-6 and Psalm 27). This simple truth can indeed incite us to rekindle and to re-ignite our relationship with the Almighty God to rise from this crisis of spiritual defeat to a place where we experience the victorious life that Jesus Christ purchased for us. Jesus died for our sins and God resurrected Him to bring us a new and victorious life!

Today, many in the Body of Christ seem to live an idolatrous and adulterous life-- forgetting God, who should be the center of our worship. However, a clarion call has gone out to the Body of Christ! The trumpet has sounded in Zion and God is telling His people to flee idolatry and run to the power of His Presence! The church, who is the Bride of Christ, has somehow forgotten about the marriage to the bridegroom (Jesus Christ) and has become betrothed to the "wisdom of man" and to other earthly, fleshly carnal desires. This abominable act has caused the church to become an adulterer. There is now a great crisis of idolatry that is causing much deception and a lack of individuals who are seeking out their God given individual purpose. Idolatry is also causing a great falling away of the assembling together by many who solely seek salvation, solitude, refuge, and the power of God through His Son Jesus Christ. Idolatry and adultery are also causing the church to settle for religion (set rules of do's, don'ts, and nominal living) instead of a desire for a relationship with God. We must return to living in accordance with the Spirit of God instead of living in accordance with our fleshly nature–the nature that only leads to death. The good news is that God stands ready to deliver us if we would humble ourselves, pray, seek His face, and turn from our wicked ways. God has called us to stay connected to Him through our worship.

OUR PERSONAL RELATIONSHIP WITH GOD

LET US LOOK AT OUR PERSONAL RELATIONSHIP WITH GOD.

I Peter 2:5 states that we are being built into a spiritual house to be a holy priesthood, offering spiritual sacrifices acceptable to God through Jesus Christ. We must focus on building up our spiritual house so that we can offer up our lives as living sacrifices, holy and acceptable to God.

> *"By wisdom, a house is built, and through understanding it is established; through knowledge its rooms are filled with rare treasures." Proverbs 24:3-4 (NIV)*

A HOUSE IS BUILT BY WISDOM.

This is the true beginning of our spiritual journey with God. Wisdom is the raw material used to build up our spiritual house. Psalm 111:10 states that the fear of the Lord is the beginning of Wisdom. In this scripture, we can define fear as both a reverential and a dreadful fear of God. When this fear is developed in our hearts, we are often consumed with a burning desire to draw closer and closer to God. We lose ourselves in the bosom of God—-and He becomes real to us. We must diligently maintain a reverential and a dreadful fear of God so that we may always decrease while the Holy Spirit increases in us. This act of respect and obeisance is the beginning of wisdom.

THE HOUSE IS ESTABLISHED THROUGH UNDERSTANDING.

As we grow, we are being built into a spiritual house to be a holy priesthood. This understanding of what Jesus has done for us establishes the boundaries of the spiritual house within us. At this phase, the testimony of Jesus Christ rises big in our lives, and we become the evidence and substance of an unseen God. Our true worship then flows from our understanding of what Jesus has done for us. He first loved us. Worship returns that love.

Revelation 1: 5-6 state that we have been freed from our sins by the blood of Jesus Christ and have been made kings and priests to serve God. I Peter 2: 2-5 declares that after we have accepted what Jesus has done for us, we are to grow up in our salvation.

THROUGH KNOWLEDGE ITS ROOMS ARE FILLED.

As we humble ourselves before God and allow Him to increase in our lives daily, we begin to experience an unbroken sweet fellowship with the Father, and we begin to know His nature and His ways. **God also begins to deposit gifts, callings, visions, and a deep spiritual knowledge and understanding of our purpose in the earth.** God then speaks into our lives, and He orders our every step. As He orders our steps, we begin to bear fruit. "True Worshipers" are fruitful because we begin to manifest who God is in the earth.

THE WORSHIP ENCOUNTER

Jesus is The Way, The Truth and The Life. He is the <u>doorway</u> that we enter to worship the Father. Jesus opened the way for us to live a life of constant worship and fellowship with the Father. The plan of Jesus' life in the earth is to lead us through and past Himself to our Father God. Jesus wants us to live the same life He lived upon earth—always looking up to, depending upon, and honoring His Father (our Father in heaven). God longs for His children to dwell in that kind of love as they delight in His presence. He sent His son to bring us to Him. Worship is the connection of our spirit to God's Spirit. During worship, we communicate with God as He speaks into our hearts.

Worship is throne-centered, and it is an overflow of our intimate fellowship with God. (We are right there with God, at His feet crying Holy even as the angels cry Holy.) It is a spontaneous response to the love that God has for us. During worship, God reveals His glory through us as He ministers to our hearts.

> *"I will ask the Father, and he will give you another Advocate to help you and be with you forever—the Spirit of truth. The world cannot accept him because it neither sees him nor knows him. But you know him, for he lives with you and will be in you. I will not leave you as orphans; I will come to you. Before long, the world will not see me anymore, but you will see me. Because I live, you also will live. On that day you will realize that I am in my Father, and you are in me, and I am in you." John 14:16-20 (NIV)*

THE RELEASE OF GOD'S GLORY

As we seek the face of God in True Worship, we must know that God is desiring to release and display His Glory in the earth. In worship, He places us under an open heaven for all eyes to clearly see Him through our lives. As He releases His Glory, this becomes the catalyst and fuel that advances His Kingdom in the earth.

Through our worship encounters, the King of Glory engages us in dramatic turning points and pivotal moments that bring radical and supernatural outcomes in the earth. Our worship encounters allow God to induce and infuse us while miracles begin to manifest in the earth. For example, impossibilities become possibilities. Our weaknesses become the strength of our God. And our unknown person begins to represent the plans and purposes of the Almighty, Eternal God in the earth.

WHAT DOES THE BIBLE SAY ABOUT THE KING GLORY?

In the Old Testament--The common Hebrew word for Glory is Kabod (Pronounced Kahvode) which means:

- heavy, weighty,

- fullness, or the full weight of something

- weightiness of someone of high importance, a person of notable, impressive, and positive reputation.

"The voice of the Lord is upon the waters: the God of glory thundereth;" **Psalm 29:3** (KJV). This Psalm reveals God's great power! Psalm 97:6 and 9 (NKJV) say: *"The heavens declare his righteousness, and all the people see His glory. For You, Lord, are most high above all the earth; You are exalted far above all gods."* The Glory of God—Kabod (pronounced Kahvode) means the visible manifestation of God; the reputation for greatness for which God alone deserves because of His miraculous actions of deliverance and Salvation. In the New Testament the common Greek Word for glory is Doxa, it is used as follows:

- to describe the nature and acts of God in self-manifestation. For example, what God does and who He is, are fully revealed.

- Doxa is the manifested perfection of God's character.

Additionally, John 1:14 (KJV) says: *"And the Word was made flesh, and dwelt among us, (and we beheld his glory, the glory as of the only begotten of the Father), full of grace and truth."* Therefore, the word Glory in both the New and Old testaments (Kabod and Doxa) can be summarized as follows:

- the weightiness of God and His reputation,

- the fullness of His presence in the earth,

- the visible manifestations of His attributes and character

26

- the full expression of His nature

God desires to put His attributes, character, and nature on display to assist, aid, and to encourage us into action. The whole earth groans and waits for the manifestation of God's Glory in the earth. *Habakkuk 2:14 (Amplified) says: "But [the time is coming when] the earth shall be filled with the knowledge of the glory of the Lord as the waters cover the sea."* According to this scripture, there is coming a time in the earth when God's Glory will make a greater demand on our lives. Therefore, we must hunger for more of His presence to usher in more of His Glory.

The Bible gives us examples of people induced by the King of Glory at critical moments in the earth to bring about God's purpose. They moved fearlessly during every tumultuous moment and was confident that the glory of God would go before them and would also be their rear guard. If we never face a problem or negative situation, we will never know the full power of God in our lives. What we may see as a problem, God sees as an opportunity to manifest His Glory. The King of Glory is waiting to release His Glory in this hour to show Himself Mighty in every chaotic situation. Therefore, we must strive to go beyond a nominal walk with God. We must also go beyond a state of "Ichabod" (the lack of God's Glory) and become carriers of His Glory in the earth.

The Bible gives an amazing example regarding a person who fearlessly displayed God's glory in the earth. This person is Jochebed, Moses' Mother whose name is mentioned only in Exodus 6:20 and Numbers 26:59. Although her son Moses, became a mighty deliverer, we rarely hear the mention of her name. However, Jochebed caused a spiritual avalanche beyond her generation. I believe that God's Glory made a demand on her life that empowered and thrusted her into a major move that extended far beyond her years. Imagine the miracles and possibilities that God could manifest through our lives.

I believe Jochebed knew that the King of Glory was about to make His tangible entrance in the earth during a time of chaos.

Psalm 24:7-10 (NKJV) state: "Lift up your heads, O ye gates! And be lifted up, you everlasting doors! And the King of glory shall come in. Who is this King of glory? The Lord strong and mighty, The Lord Mighty in battle, the Lord of Host. He is the King of Glory". Jochebed knew that God was waiting to demonstrate His authority, His Power, His greatness, weightiness, and the fullness of His Presence in the Earth. His Reputation of deliverance and Salvation was about to go on display for all men to see. Although seeking God's presence leads to the manifestation of His Glory, when His Glory makes a demand on our lives, all of God's attributes and character begin to go on display. He begins to expose His nature and Power. He allows us to visibly see Him at Work. God's presence is invisible. However, His Glory is tangible. It can be seen and observed. Like Jochebed, worshipers must take our reputation and ourselves out of the equation and welcome the reputation of the King. We must boast of His greatness and weightiness as we welcome Him and carry His glory to a lost, dying, and chaotic world.

Jochebed's name in the Hebrew language means "God's glory" "glory of Jehovah" or "Jehovah is our glory." She knew the purpose of her name and how God could use her life in the earth. Therefore, I believe that she also understood and welcomed the visible manifestation of God through her life. Jochebed was far into her pregnancy with her third child when Pharaoh (the oppressor) made an edict that all newly born Hebrew boys should be thrown in the Nile. She risked her family's life and began to radically fight for her baby's life. When Moses was born (See Exodus 2:2, Acts 7:20 and Hebrews 11:23), Jochebed saw that Moses was a special child who was favored (God's Grace was upon Him). She knew that Moses was sent from God with Divine purpose just like she was sent from God to carry His Glory. She believed that the King of Glory would manifest and preserve the child. By faith, Jochebed hid Moses for three months, built him an ark of safety, and put him in the river. The rest is history. Jochebed's baby boy became one the greatest leaders and deliverers the world has ever known. When God's Glory makes a demand on our lives, purpose is transformed into movement. Our Faith and trust are activated, and we become fueled and driven by God.

God responds to us according to the proportion of the hunger and thirst in our hearts. Let us draw nearer to Him. God is still seeking True Worshipers in this hour who are bold enough to allow Him to display His glory through our lives.

SELAH (PAUSE AND CALMLY THINK ABOUT IT). HOW DO WE PREPARE OUR HEART TO ENCOUNTER GOD IN TRUE WORSHIP?

(1) Come humbly. Humility, Humility, Humility is the key word. First, enter the gates of God with Thanksgiving. Thank Him for every waking moment. Have a heart of gratitude for who God is and for what He has done in your life. Then enter God's courts with praise. Exalt and extol His name. For example, speak to Him and tell Him that He is Highest God, the Most High, Elohiym (the Hebrew name of God that means Creator and Judge of the universe), Jesus, Lord of lords, and King of kings, The I AM that I AM. Now thank God for receiving your sacrifice of praise unto Him and believe that God will consume your praise and bring you into "True Worship." This is a place of deep humility. As we humble ourselves before God and allow Him to increase in our lives daily, we begin to experience an unbroken sweet fellowship with the Father. This is where worship takes place. Humility prevents us from falling into the same trap that Lucifer fell into. (The sin of Lucifer was pride and the inability to market the Word of God (he refused to obey and do what God desired him to do).

> *"Because the foolishness of God is wiser than men, and the weakness of God is stronger than men. For you see your calling, brethren, that not many wise according to the flesh, not many mighty, not many noble, are called. But God has chosen the foolish things of the world to put to shame the wise, and God has chosen the*

weak things of the world to put to shame the things which are mighty; and the base things of the world and the things which are despised God has chosen, and the things which are not, to bring to nothing the things that are, that no flesh should glory in His presence. I Corinthians 1: 25-29 (NKJV)

(2) Have a constant desire to draw near to God and to behold His beauty.

(3) Read the Word of God daily and inquire of God for a full understanding of His ways (Hebrews 10: 19-23 and Psalm 27:4).

(4) Pray in the Spirit daily. (Desire the baptism of the Holy Spirit and pray in the spirit. The book of Jude tells us to build yourselves up in your most Holy faith—praying in the Holy Spirit).

(5) Simply yield to the "Spirit of God" within.

(6) Desire for others to know the whole measure of the fullness of Christ (Ephesians 4:13).

(7) Fully obey the Word of God not by mere talk but by action.

God's plan in the New Testament is that we worship Him more intensely than those in the Old Testament because the kingdom of heaven is within us. Ephesians 2:6 tells us that God raised us up with Christ and seated us with Him in heavenly places. *Colossians 3:1-4 (NKJV -paraphrased) tell us that if we are raised with Christ, seek those things which are above, where Christ sits on the right hand of God. Set your mind and affection on things above, not on things on the earth. For you died, and your life is hidden with Christ in God. When Christ, who is our life, shall appear, then we shall appear with Him in glory.* Therefore, let us give true testimony to Christ and worship God! Let us bring heaven to earth. ***Our Father which art in heaven, Hallowed be thy name. Thy Kingdom Come! Thy will be done on earth as it is in Heaven!***

SUMMARY, REVIEW, AND PERSONAL REFLECTIONS

1. In your own words, what is the meaning of John 4:23-24?

2. What is True Worship, and what is not True Worship?

3. What is idolatry?

4. Why do we worship God?

5. Why is it important to practice the presence of God daily?

6. What are specific Hebrew and Greek definitions of Worship? How can you implement these definitions in your life?

7. Give specific examples of worshipers in the Bible.

8. How did these individuals worship God with their lives and what can we learn from their lives?

9. Explain the release of God's Glory in the earth.

Lastly, I recommend a daily practice of the presence of God in true silence without any distractions. Lay prostrate (facedown) before God and shut out the world for a moment. Listen to the voice of God as He speaks into your spirit man. Keep a journal and plan your time with Him. Before you know it, you will become addicted to this place of deep intimate love of God and with God. My prayer is that you will become seeker magnetic and forever desire to live in an unbroken fellowship with God as He manifests in your life in ways you never imagined.

NOTES

(This page is intentionally left blank for note taking)

EFFECTUAL FERVENT PRAYER

EFFECTUAL FERVENT PRAYER

GOAL

The goal of this section is to present "Effectual Fervent Prayer" as one of the ways to walk in Kingdom dominion authority. This section is radical, yet informative and will take your prayers and intercessions to a higher level. If you also desire to teach about intercessory prayer, this section will provide you with essential and valuable information to use in your instructions.

WHAT YOU WILL NEED TO GET STARTED

To receive the greatest benefit from this section, I suggest the following:

a. A teachable, honest, and yielded heart,

b. Willingness to take a radical stance in your life and for the lives of others,

c. Obedience and surrender to the call as an intercessor,

d. A desire to engage in consistent prayers and intercession,

e. A willingness to use your voice to make declarations and decrees in the earth.

f. I also recommend that you start or join a prayer group of like-minded believers to come in agreement with your prayers and intercessions. Leading or joining a corporate prayer group will also aid in your growth as a prayer warrior and intercessor. Remember, "THE EFFECTUAL FERVENT PRAYERS OF A RIGHTEOUS MAN AVAILETH MUCH!"

THE INTERCESSOR AND EFFECTUAL FERVENT PRAYER

We must first focus on introspection (looking inwardly and being truthful) before we can have effectual fervent prayer. Without the effectual fervent prayer of a **righteous man,** much cannot be availed. Therefore, we must be properly aligned with the Father in a deep intimate relationship with Him to hear and receive His guidance and direction through prayer. The Bible tells us about the seven sons of Sceva who did not know Jesus personally and were whipped and defeated by demons (See Acts 19:14). The sons of Sceva did not have a proper relationship with God. When they tried to mimic what other believers were doing, they were defeated. Therefore, intercessory prayer is not just something we do because others are doing it. "We must become intercessors." We must be pure before God. *Psalm 24:3-4 (NKJV) asks, "Who may ascend into the hill of the Lord? Or who may stand in His holy place? He who has clean hands and a pure heart".*

The effectual fervent prayer of a righteous man availeth much." James 5:16(b) (KJV). In the verse, "availeth" comes from the Greek word Ischuo [pronounced is-khoo-o]. It means to have or exercise force, to be strong, to have efficacy, force, or value, to prevail. This term indicates a more forceful strength than the word dunamai (another Greek word) which in contrast is "potential" or a state of being, while Ischuo means kinetic action or action in motion. It is also important to note that James said availeth much—which clearly magnifies the power, force, strength, and efficacy of the righteous man's prayer. This is prayer that will boldly engage the enemy, resist him, keep him under our feet, and send him back to the pit where he belongs.

WHAT IS INTERCESSORY PRAYER?

Intercessory prayer is:

1. **VIOLENTLY WAGING SPIRITUAL WARFARE** against the enemy's devices. The plan of the enemy is evident in John 10:10 which tells us that the enemy comes but to steal, kill, and to destroy. But Jesus counteracted this plan by bringing us life and life more abundantly. Our Kingdom life here on earth, is a life of authority and dominion. Therefore, we must fight the good fight of faith and wage war against anything that comes to kill, steal, and destroy.

   Additionally, it is my belief from studying the Bible, that John the Baptist was radical? Yet, the Bible tells us that he who is least in the Kingdom of heaven is greater than John. This means that those of us in God's Kingdom are more than radical...

   > *"Assuredly I say to you, among those born of women there has not risen one greater than John the Baptist; but he who is least in the Kingdom of heaven is greater than he. And from the days of John the Baptist until now, the kingdom of heaven suffers violence.... and the violent take it by force.... Matthew 11:11-and 12 (NKJV)*

The scriptures call us VIOLENT. Are you fed up with all the crazy attacks from the enemy? Have you had enough yet? Well, it is time to get violent. It is time to get hell's attention. You cannot just sit quiet. Do not just take the enemy's attacks while lying down—Get up and take God's Kingdom by force and walk in your Kingdom dominion authority! The intercessor violently wages war against the devices of the devil through effectual fervent prayer. This includes the use of the Word of God and the assistance of the Holy Spirit. After Jesus ascended back to the Father, God sent His precious Holy Spirit to empower us to walk as His witnesses in the earth. Therefore, it is vital that we remain connected to the Holy

Spirit, our power source, while we pray. Jude 1 tells us to build ourselves up in our most holy faith, praying in the Holy Spirit.

2. <u>**STANDING IN THE GAP AND MAKING UP THE HEDGE.**</u>

THE DYING WORLD NEEDS US…TO STAND IN THE GAP AND MAKE UP THE HEDGE for individuals, families, cities, states, nations, and the world. Standing in the gap and making up the hedge mean that we become THE BRIDGE…AND THE SURROUNDING WALL OF PROTECTION for others SO THAT THE GATES OF HELL WOULD NOT PREVAIL. Everything that has broken away from God or is separated from God, **needs an INTERCESSOR WHO WILL TRAVAIL as that "bridge" until change comes**. Travail means that we bombard heaven and we put God in remembrance of His Word while we cry out to Him to intervene in specific affairs.

> *(Ezekiel 22:30 KJV) says: ("I sought for a MAN among them, that should make up the hedge, and stand in the gap before me for the land, that I should not destroy it: but I found none)."* **ARE YOU AVAILABLE TO THE LORD?**

3. <u>**BECOMING THE REPAIRER OF THE BREACH AND RESTORER OF STREETS TO DWELL IN.**</u>

This means that through intercession, we serve as THE RETAINING WALLS BUILT BY A MASON…the mortar, the bricks, the stones, the granite the exceptionally durable structure THAT HOLDS UP AND RENEWS ANY THING THAT IS dilapidated, broken away, scattered, or worn down by the enemy. We do all of this while <u>bringing about repentance, deliverance, and rescue of others from the very pit of hell!</u> Remember that the "Now I lay me down to sleep" types of prayers are not enough and will never do the job as an intercessor—those nominal prayers are not enough for those serious about repairing breaches and restoring broken places in the earth. We must powerfully use the Word of God to breathe life into every broken place as we declare and decree life, Salvation, wholeness, and restoration!

(Isaiah 58:12 NKJV) says: *"You shall be called Repairer of the Breach, The Restorer of STREETS to Dwell in."*

4. <u>**TAKING OUR ROLE AS WATCHMEN ON THE WALL.**</u>

As an intercessor, we set up guard, protect, observe, keep, and preserve. <u>WE NEVER STOP PETITIONING GOD UNTIL CHANGE COMES</u>. Watchmen are like enforcement officers who are not paranoid. Although they are challenged daily as evil lurks in our communities, enforcement officers relentlessly patrol, conduct surprise stops and checks, and sometimes just reveal the force of their authority by observing and making their presence known.

(Isaiah 62:6-7 NKJV) say: "I have set watchmen on your walls, O Jerusalem; They shall never hold their peace day or night. You who make mention of the Lord, do not keep silent, and give Him no rest till He establishes and till He makes Jerusalem a praise in the earth."

Similarly, as watchmen on the wall…WE MUST LEARN TO STAY IN THE FACE OF GOD UNTIL WE SEE CHANGE…As citizens of God's Kingdom, we ENFORCE GOD'S AUTHORITY HERE ON EARTH.

Matthew 16:19 in the Amplified Bible states: "I will give you the keys to the Kingdom of Heaven, and whatever you bind on earth, (declare to be improper and unlawful) on the earth must be what is already bound in heaven. And whatever you loose (declare lawful) on earth must be what is already loosed in heaven."

These scriptures describe God's plan for us as Kingdom Citizens who are always conscious of bringing heaven to earth. As watchmen, we are constantly declaring and ensuring that God's Kingdom has come, and His will is done in the earth. Intercessors, never leave your position! The enemy stays with his role (of accusing the brethren and constantly trying to make us feel defeated). Therefore, we must become watchmen on the wall as we continuously use our spiritual weapons of war. How do we stay in our position? Let us look at this example in the Word of God.

OCCUPY AND ENGAGE THE VICTORY WON BY JESUS CHRIST

This is how we continuously engage our victory! In the natural, a military government is the government <u>established by a military commander in conquered territory. The military commander</u> administers the military law declared by him under military authority applicable to all persons in the conquered territory. These military laws supersede any incompatible local law. This government then occupies the territory and ensures victory. Similarly, in God's Kingdom we have already won. Therefore, we live in, occupy, and maintain, conquered territory and we must declare this ONGOING VICTORY because *<u>Colossians 2:15 (NKJV) tells us that Jesus Christ</u>—disarmed and dismantled satan and all evil forces… "Having disarmed principalities and powers, He made a public spectacle of them, triumphing over them in it." (<u>The KJV says: having spoiled</u>—*The Greek word for "spoiled" is pronounced apekdoo-om-ahee; (and spelled apekduomai). This word means to strip off clothes or armaments. Jesus took away all satan's weapons, artilleries, his guns, and the effectiveness of the enemy's mobilizations and moves. Our job is to occupy and maintain God's Kingdom until Jesus Christ returns.

Isaiah 54:17 (NKJV) prepared us for this position by stating that *"No weapon formed against you shall proper, And every tongue which rises against you in judgment You shall condemn. This is the heritage of the servants of the Lord, And their righteousness is from Me, Says the Lord."* Also, John 14:12 (NKJV) says: *"…he who believes in Me, the works that I do, he will do also; and greater works than these he will do, because I go to My Father".* We are representatives of the victory won by Christ in the earth. If we believe that we already won, we must acknowledge that the enemy is trespassing when he rears his ugly head. Then, we must take our stand through Christ, and declare the enemy a public spectacle. God wants us to keep our eyes on the VICTORY!

God is calling us to "Occupy" the conquered territory of the Kingdom until His Son Jesus the Christ returns. Let us look at Luke 19:13-24 (KJV). This passage reads:

[13] *And he called his ten servants, and delivered them ten pounds, and said unto them, Occupy till I come.*

[14] *But his citizens hated him, and sent a message after him, saying, we will not have this man to reign over us.*

[15] *And it came to pass, that when he was returned, having received the kingdom, then he commanded these servants to be called unto him, to whom he had given the money, that he might know how much every man had gained by trading.*

[16] *Then came the first, saying, Lord, thy pound hath gained ten pounds.*

[17] *And he said unto him, well, thou good servant: because thou hast been faithful in a very little, have thou authority over ten cities.*

[18] *And the second came, saying, Lord, thy pound hath gained five pounds.*

[19] *And he said likewise to him, Be thou also over five cities.*

²⁰ And another came, saying, Lord, behold, here is thy pound, which I have kept laid up in a napkin:

²¹ For I feared thee, because thou art an austere man: thou takest up that thou layedst not down, and reapest that thou didst not sow.

²² And he saith unto him, out of thine own mouth will I judge thee, thou wicked servant. Thou knewest that I was an austere man, taking up that I laid not down, and reaping that I did not sow:

²³ Wherefore then gavest not thou my money into the bank, that at my coming I might have required mine own with usury?

²⁴ And he said unto them that stood by, take from him the pound, and give it to him that hath ten pounds."

Often, we read or study this parable and we focus only on the servant that did not do anything with the money or investment that was given to him and that those that increased the investment were rewarded more. However, this passage starts with a command– **"OCCUPY UNTIL I COME."** Many times, we read the Word of God a little too fast and sometimes miss the important nuggets found in the Bible. Nonetheless, let us examine what this parable is commanding us to do. "Occupy" in the Greek is the word pragmateuomai pronounced prag-mat-yoo-omahee and it means:

- To Busy oneself (Many times when we hear the word occupy in the English language, we think that our role is merely to just lodge around and inhabit something—like a couch potato or slothful person.) Think about it for a moment. What is your vision of occupy? Is it just sitting there as if you are waiting for something to go down?

- Clearly the definition tells us that "Occupy" means to busy oneself; to engage in business—God wants us to get busy in His

Kingdom…He made a mighty investment of LOVE TO US –by giving His Son Jesus Christ. *"For God so loved the World that He gave His only begotten Son."* God expects and commands us to multiply what Jesus did in the earth. We must multiply the love of God in the earth by making disciples of all Nations. (See John 3:16 and Matthew 28:18-20 in the Amplified Bible.)

- The Word occupy is derived from two root words Pragma and Prasso which mean: to do; to practice; perform repeatedly or habitually (not a single act); to execute; accomplish; commit.

We engage our "Victory" by being proactive and intentional in God's Kingdom. One of the Greek definitions of "occupy" says to perform repeatedly— (Believers may have said out of frustration: "Well I witnessed, and no one accepted Christ") or ("those people told me that they were coming to church, and they didn't show up.") So often we become paralyzed and lifeless frustrated believers because we are looking for results from our one time or limited acts. Although we must do our part in God's Kingdom, remember that God is the Lord of the Harvest. We are the laborers who go out and walk in obedience in God's Kingdom. We plant and we water, but it is God who gives the increase. We occupy by continuing to plant and to water. God will surely bring the increase.

God is reminding us that He invested His dunamis (This is a Greek word that means power) and exousia (This is a Greek word that means authoriity) in us through His Son Jesus Christ (See Ephesians 1:19 through 23). When God raised Jesus from the dead, He made Him the head and we are the Body…who must engage in Kingdom business. Woe unto us if we look to the sky for a rapture to take us out of the world and not multiply the "power" investment that God gave us. Woe unto us if we just sit back declaring that we are Christians instead of snatching sinners out of the fire while hating their very clothing stained with sin (Jude 1:23).

The Holy Spirit wants us to see that "Occupying"—includes action. Do not grow weary now, allow the power of God that comes from the resurrected Christ to overflow in your lives. The Body of Christ is in a critical time in the earth—with all the chaos, opposition, and apparent increase of evil and wickedness. However, it is important to note that all great revivals and awakenings of the PAST came about because the Body of Christ found itself at a tipping point (the point that pushed believers right into a mighty move of God!) The word "TILL" or "UNTIL" noted in Luke 19:13 is defined in the Greek as "to not grow weary. "

- This Greek word is "Heos" and pronounced (Hey-oce). Till or until also expresses a relation of time, circumstance, manner, cause, or degree.

- "Heos" is also a conjunction and a preposition meaning: until, as far as, up to, as much as.

Here, we are encouraged not to stop but to continue occupying the Kingdom of God up to the time when Jesus Christ returns. Never quit because, true winners never quit, and quitters can never win or enjoy the victory. At the Walls of Salvation Church Ministries, we say it like this: "I cannot stop; I will not stop; until I reach my promised land."

HOW TO TAKE AUTHORITY OVER THE SPIRITUAL REALM

WE MUST ACKNOWLEDGE THE EXISTENCE OF THE SPIRITUAL REALM AND TAKE AUTHORITY OVER IT!

> II Corinthians 10:3-5 say (NKJV): *"though we walk in the flesh, we do not war according to the flesh. For the weapons of our warfare are not carnal but mighty in God for pulling down strongholds, casting down arguments and every high thing that exalts itself against*

the knowledge of God, bringing every thought into captivity to the obedience of Christ"

THIS IS WHAT I CALL OUR 10:4 SPIRITUAL WEAPON. We declare to the devil..."OVER AND OUT"!.... We cannot wish that a stronghold would just go away or disappear, we must engage in spiritual warfare and use our mighty weapons given by God.

Unfortunately, some people do not believe that the spiritual realm is real. However, if anyone picks up the newspaper or turns on the television and looks at the current events, many of us would easily identify the number of demonic influences in our culture. The spiritual realm is real and alive. As leaders, we cannot take pleasure in these demonic activities, or we will quench the Spirit and Power of God within us. **THE DYING WORLD NEEDS US—TO PRAY** Effectually and Fervently against all demonic influences.

EXERCISE & TAKE AUTHORITY IN THE SPIRIT WORLD AROUND YOU!

1. "Pray always with all prayer and supplication in the Spirit and watching thereunto with all perseverance and supplication for all saints." (See Ephesians 6:18 – KJV)

2. "For this purpose the Son of God was manifested, that He might destroy the works of the devil." (I John 3:8 -KJV) Know that Jesus came and already defeated the works of the devil. Therefore, let us continue to enforce the defeat of our enemy.

3. Know and exercise the principles and keys of the Kingdom of God. (Matthew 16:19 KJV, Binding and loosing--declaring what is legal and illegal in the earth as it is in heaven).

4. Get and stay on the offense with a mind to score in God's Kingdom. Do not be slothful and reactive to the enemy's strategies...Be rather proactive and identify and resist him before he

plots and strikes. (Pray daily for Divine Healing, Divine Health, and a Divine Life).

5. Know that we are more than conquerors through Christ Jesus who loved us (Romans 8:37 – KJV).

KNOW AND DEFEAT THE STRONGMEN

Know and defeat the 12 strongmen under whom most demonic activity exists. A knowledge of these strongmen will help us identify the types of attacks that the enemy uses in the earth. Once identified, we can shine God's light into these dark areas and defeat the enemy and his strategies. In Matthew 28:18, Jesus says: ...*All power is given unto me in heaven and on earth...go therefore...* We must enforce God's authority here on earth as believers of Christ.

Luke 10:19 says, "Behold, I give unto you power to tread on serpents and scorpions, and over all the power of the enemy: and nothing shall by any means hurt you."

12 TYPES OF STRONGMEN

1. SPIRIT OF JEALOUSY – This spirit manifests by rage, anger, and suspicion, murder, revenge, vengeance (See Numbers 5:11-14 – Spirit of Jealousy). We see this just by watching the news. This spirit is exemplified by gang violence and other types of killings. This includes raging individuals who are snapping and killing thoughtlessly (Not just in a physical sense). Additionally, hurt, and bruised people can become highly emotional resulting in actions that also kill the dreams, passions, ambitions, and excitement of others.

2. <u>LYING SPIRIT</u> – This spirit manifests by all religious spirits. It is a fake spirit that can manifests with fake tongues (This can be a manifestation of someone pretending to be baptized in the Holy Spirit, but instead is making fake sounds that may be high pitched and babbling.) The <u>action of the person is to make others think that they know God – one may think that the person is of God unless one can discern otherwise</u>. The religious spirit is a very filthy spirit. It is a stubborn, controlling, and forceful spirit. It often manifests as always right---people do not feel comfortable around this person if they are not in their clicks. This person always says "God says" … The person with the religious spirit may appear somewhat batty and crazy. (See Jeremiah 23:14-16 and Ezekiel 24:9-12 KJV).

3. <u>FAMILIAR SPIRIT</u> – (See I Samuel 28:7) This is the <u>spirit of divination appearing as a familiar spirit</u>. This is often manifested in individuals who act exceptionally holy and as though they know the future…through Astrology and fortune telling (See Deut. 18: 10-12). This is evident in all the psychic little places we see everywhere and the witchcraft that dominates the TV and appear in movies. This is also evident in people who conduct séances and similar activities. All the stories of dead loved ones who reappear are familiar demonic spirits AND are NOT OF GOD! Do not entertain them. Rebuke and reject every familiar spirit in Jesus' name.

4. <u>PERVERT SPIRIT</u> – This spirit includes all kinds of perversion or deviation from God's truth. See Isaiah 19:14, Proverbs. 14:2 (KJV) This includes all forms of lust. Prov. 23:33 (KJV). This person lives a complete lie. (Acts 13:10 (KJV). The person twists the Bible to fit their lifestyle. This spirit controls all homosexuality and same-sex attraction. <u>It hates God and causes people to live a lie. It is a very convincing spirit. Everything the person says is a</u>

lie. This is one of the strongest demons because it often uses the Bible out of context to prove it is right.

5. SPIRIT OF WHOREDOM – This spirit manifests by prostitution, idolatry, and by people bound to ALL TYPES OF HABITS such as soap operas, TV shows, video games, and social media. (See Hosea 4:12 Ezekiel 16:28-39).

6. SPIRIT OF HEAVINESS – (See Isaiah 61:3) This spirit manifests by despair and gloominess, grief, hopelessness, depression, and rejection. Individuals with this spirit of heaviness may sleep more than usual to forget or block out the heaviness. Also, this spirit often comes from severe trauma and emotional abuse. Today, many are becoming despondent because of the crushing cares of this world and are losing their minds because of this spirit of heaviness. We must defeat this spirit. Isaiah 61:3 tells us that we can put on the garment of praise instead of the spirit of heaviness.

7. SPIRIT OF INFIRMITY – (See Luke 13:11) This spirit includes all sickness and diseases manifesting in our body....we can see this spirit dominating as the overall well-being of our country appears to be facing a decline...in many cases, this spirit of infirmity is caused by the greed of other men who are trying to get rich at the expense of society's health. This includes overuse and addiction to Opioids, overdose of prescription drugs...toxic food systems that include genetically modified and cloned foods as well as all types of manufactured food that have been artificially produced etc. Today, there are investigative cases of doctors being arrested for intentionally overdosing and illegally prescribing medications. Many of these practices bring about a spirit of infirmity in our society.

8. DEAF AND DUMB SPIRIT – (See Mark 9:17-25) (KJV) This spirit manifests by epilepsy, seizures, anorexia (refusing to eat)

suicide, and lunacy. It seems like we are living in a society where people are going crazy and insane everywhere. In some cases, this spirit is treated as normal and as just a health issue that needs to be medicated. This spirit is also manifested in the many heinous acts of even parents killing their own children etc. Matthew 17:14-21 (KJV).

9. <u>SPIRIT OF FEAR</u> – (See II Timothy 1:7) (KJV) This spirit manifests by constant torment, terror, inferiority, phobias (such as height and the dark). This spirit often causes nightmares. Job 4:14 (KJV).

10. <u>SPIRIT OF PRIDE</u> – (See Proverbs 16:18) This spirit manifests by fighting and contention. Proverbs 13:10, Prov. 21:24. It also manifests in "Self-Righteousness" and in a person who appears controlling. (Lucifer had a spirit of pride and he was eternally assigned to hell).

11. <u>DEVIL (or SPIRIT) OF BONDAGE</u> (See Romans 8:15) This spirit manifests by all addictions and many of the traps and snares that we cannot seem to shake off. (For example, this includes drug addiction, sex addiction, pornography, and video gaming obsession).

12. <u>DEVIL (or SPRITI) OF ANTICHRIST</u> – (See I John 4:3, I John 2:18) This spirit manifests by all who are against Jesus Christ and against the nations that believe in Jesus Christ. This spirit is clearly on the rise. Many false religions are rising while Christians seem to be shrinking back.

HOW DO WE INTERCEDE?

INTERCESSORY PRAYER IS TAKING AUTHORITY OVER THE SPIRITUAL REALM

KNOW THAT WE ARE NOT ALONE

> *"And I will ask the Father, and He will give you another Comforter (this scripture further says: --Counselor, Helper, Intercessor, Advocate, Strengthener, and Standby that He may remain with you forever) the Spirit of Truth (the Holy Spirit of God)..." John 14:16 in the Amplified Bible*

This scripture tells us that the Chief Intercessor resides in us, and we are not out in the deep somewhere praying our own prayers. As we grow closer in a deep intimate relationship with the Holy Spirit of God, we will know His very heartbeat, will, and concerns and we will act as a co-laborer. Our role is to become vessels who give God legal access in the earth as we enforce God's authority.

USE OUR SPIRITUAL WEAPONS OF WAR:

(1) POSITION YOURSELF IN RIGHT STANDING WITH GOD

We must first ensure that our prayers are not hindered. (PUT ON THE righteousness of God in Christ Jesus NOT OUR OWN RIGHTEOUSNESS OR WE may be defeated LIKE THE SEVEN SONS OF SCEVA (See Acts 19:14-17).

Also read II Chronicles 7:14 (NKJV) and allow this scripture to become a reality.

> *"If my people who are called by my name will humble themselves, and pray and seek my face and turn from their wicked ways, then I will hear from heaven and will forgive their sin and heal their land."*

To position ourselves in right standing with God, we must look inwardly by first turning down the plate (fast the flesh and feed the spirit man) to allow our prayers to avail. We must walk by the Spirit and always remember that *"It is not by might nor by power but by MY Spirit, says the Lord of Hosts (See Zechariah 4:6 NKJV)."* We must learn to be consumed with the fire of God's Spirit and allow the fire of God to consume and quench every fiery dart of the wicked one.

(2) USE THE WORD OF GOD

USE the Keys of the Kingdom and EVERY PROMISE THAT GOD HAS GIVEN US in the Bible. We must GET ON THE OFFENSIVE SIDE BY KNOWING THE WORD INSIDE OUT. (NOT JUST MEMORIZING THE WORD, BUT THE WORD MUST BECOME FLESH IN OUR LIVES). The Word of God must become a tangible part of us.

Matthew 16:19 (Amplified) says: I will give you the keys to the kingdom of heaven; and whatever you bind (declare to be improper and unlawful) on earth must be what is already bound in heaven: and whatever you loose (declare lawful) on earth must be what is already loosed in heaven.

(3) PUT ON THE ARMOR OF GOD

God has given us the Armor as stated in (Ephesians 6:10-18-KJV).

a.   We must be strong in the Lord and in the power of His might

b.   Put on the whole armor (put on the entire armor and know that partial obedience is gross disobedience) that you may be able to stand against the wiles of the devil and that you may be able to withstand in the evil day.

c.   Having done all, to stand, stand therefore with your

    i.   Loins girt about with truth,

    ii.   Having on the breastplate of righteousness,

   iii.   Your feet shod with the preparation of the gospel of peace,

   iv.   Taking the shield of faith, to quench all the fiery darts of the wicked,

   v.   Take the helmet of salvation,

   vi.   and the sword of the Spirit, which is the Word of God.

In addition to the amor mentioned in Ephesians 6, there are other parts of God's Armor mentioned throughout the Bible that we should also put on. All the parts of God's amor are critical if we are going to persevere in our Faith. Let's look at two other parts of the Armor: (1) the "cloak of zeal" and (2) the "Buckler"

The Cloak of Zeal—is found in Isaiah 59:17 (KJV) "*.... He put on the garments of vengeance for clothing, and was clad with zeal as a cloak." Also, Jesus mentions ZEAL...in Revelation 3:19 (KJV). This passage says: "Be zealous therefore, and repent."* Jesus said this as He addressed the Laodicean church or the Lukewarm church...In other words, He was saying that the lack of "zeal" is a sin. We must be zealous. God is expecting us to cloak ourselves with zeal until Jesus returns.

ZEAL means:

- Having a Jealousy for the THINGS OF GOD (to protect and guard the things of God.)

- Having fervor, an eager desire or endeavor, an enthusiastic diligence, drive, devotion, and determination.

Historically, the "Officers" of Roman soldiers wore a cloak to distinguish them from other soldiers as they led the way with authority. Therefore, it can be said that the cloak of zeal distinguishes us from "lukewarm" believers who are not fully sold out to God's Kingdom. Our cloak makes us visible to the devil who trembles and flees when we show up. I believe that our cloak also distinguishes us as disciples of Christ who are truly ready to occupy "until" Jesus returns.

Another part of God's amor is the "**Buckler**." Neither the Cloak of Zeal nor the Buckler are mentioned in Ephesians 6, however, these are key parts of our amor. They are both used to keep us advancing in Kingdom dominion authority. These parts also keep us in forward motion as believers, prayer warriors, and intercessors.

The Buckler is mentioned in Psalm 91:4, Psalm 35:2, (KJV)

Then Psalm 18:2 and 30, Proverbs 2:7 and 2 Samuel 22:31 (KJV) tell us that God HIMSELF is the Buckler. What is God saying to us about this part of the amor? My research of the Roman Soldier informed me these soldiers were highly skilled in warfare and they used both a shield and a buckler. One piece was larger than the other. My research revealed that the shield and buckler were not just used to stop "darts," blows or whatever else was sent their way by the opponent or enemy. Although these parts of the armor were used as defensive weapons, they were also used offensively. In other words, they were not used passively to just stop something. Like we often say: "Oh I am using my shield of Faith or here is my buckler to quench the darts of the wicked one." On the contrary, these parts of the amor were used to **fend off, block, ricochet, and deflect**—the enemy. Soldiers used them to send back to the sender what came to bring destruction.

> **These parts of the armor were used aggressively to strike, push, trap, and pin—as well as defend.**

Bucklers were used offensively as well as defensively to charge the enemy, to strike him, to send him back, and to set him up for a blow that would kill him or ward him off.

Although the Buckler seemed to a be like a small shield and was not meant for blocking large arrows or other large projectiles from the Roman soldier, the Buckler is not to be taken for granted or downplayed. The Buckler was small because it was mostly used for easy access in everyday battle. The Buckler was used for battles that were encountered every day.

(Take another Selah Moment-Pause and think about it).

Holy Spirit is reminding us that we are to use the Buckler to "stay in action" every day as we engage the enemy. We must know that God is our Buckler, and He never leaves us or forsakes us.

> *"For thy sake we are put to death all the day long; we are regarded and counted as sheep for the slaughter. Yet amid all these things we are more than conquerors and gain a surpassing victory through Him Who loved us." Romans 8:36-37 (Amplified Bible).*

Lastly, in my research, soldiers did not just use Bucklers…but a Buckler was also a civilian weapon. The ordinary person used them. GOD is our Buckler. Whether you are a Minister, Leader, a lay person, carry your Buckler. We all need our Buckler (God with us) daily. Take time daily to invite God into your life and into all your affairs. Let us declare right now—Intervene Lord God—Intervene! We need the Buckler in church and outside of church. Every believer needs the Buckler to constantly push the enemy out of our pathway, to send the enemy back to the pit of hell 60,000 feet or more below the earth as we advance the Kingdom of God in the earth. Say out loud--**GOD IS MY BUCKLER**! I am carrying Him with me today. I will never leave home without Him. He is in me, with me and upon me. We must acknowledge that God is with us daily. We must equip ourselves daily with His presence for whatever we may face.

We need to put on the entire armor of God daily. The amor of God gives us the endurance to pray always with all prayers and supplication in the Spirit and watching thereunto with all perseverance and supplication for all saints.

(4) OFFER CONTINUAL PRAISES UNTO GOD

The Bible says that the Lord inhabits or lives in our praise. Praise invites God into our situations and circumstances. Our praises declare that we trust God despite our circumstances. God comes and consumes our sacrifice of praise and takes us into a place of worship with Him. It is important to know that in worship we often sense His tangible presence. We know that God is not about a feeling because He is available, and He is close to us whether we feel Him or not. However, His tangible presence is the weighty gel of His anointing confirming that the Chief Intercessor is with us and is strengthening us to endure. Hallelujah!

Also, Psalm 149 (KJV) says that our high praise executes vengeance upon the heathens, binds up their kings with chains, and their nobles with fetters of iron. (Our praise is a powerful weapon of war that can be used as we intercede. God inhabits or lives in our praises—Psalm 22:3). I recommend that every reader obtain a copy of my "I AM" Poster or the "I AM" (Spoken Word) audio which will encourage you to offer daily continual praises unto God." (Visit www.wallsofsalvation.global to find out how to obtain a copy). This poster and audio declare more than 100 names and attributes of God that we can decree as we Praise God. For example, we can declare that He is our Father, the I AM, Master, Mighty God, Maker of Heaven and Earth, My Salvation, Keeper, Lily in my valleys, The Way, The Truth, and The Life, Dayspring from on High, Chief Intercessor, Author and Finisher of my Faith, The Kingdom, Power, and the Glory, The Amen. These are just a few names that we can use to praise our God. There are not enough words and names to fully express our praises to God. However, as we praise and exalt God, know that the

Name of the of the Lord is a strong tower that rises above every earthly dominion and every name that is named in heaven and in earth. The righteous can run into "It" and they are safe (See Proverbs 18:10 KJV).

Intercessors and prayer warriors, I encourage you to use all your spiritual weapons of war as you take authority over the spiritual realm. Remember to position yourself in right standing with God. Use the Word of God and always put on the armor of God. Lastly, offer continual praises onto God.

KNOW YOUR IDENTITY IN GOD'S KINGDOM

We must know our Kingdom identity and ability in God's Kingdom. Walls of Salvation Church Ministries' Ambassador's confession remind us that Jesus has made us Kings and Priests unto His God and Father (Revelation 1:6). In God's Kingdom, we are more than conquerors. Therefore, we must know who we are, TAKE OUR POSITION, AND WALK IN AUTHORITY! Here are some excerpts of the Ambassadors' Confession used at the Walls of Salvation Church Ministries. I encourage every reader to make this confession. Also study the relevant scriptures that accommodate each paragraph of the confession and walk in God's authority as a powerful prayer warrior and intercessor.

WHO ARE WE IN THE KINGDOM OF GOD?

I Am a Manifested Son of God, And If a Son, Then an Heir and A Joint Heir with Jesus Christ! Jesus Christ Washed Me from My Sins by His Own Blood and Has Made Me A King and A Priest unto His God and Father. In God's Kingdom, I Am More Than a Conqueror. I Am Christ's Ambassador!

(Rom. 8, II Corinth. 6, Gal. 4, I John 3, Rev. 1, II Corinth. 5, Eph. 6:20)

I Am Abraham's Seed. I Am Blessed to Be a Blessing! I Stopped the Curse. The Curse Has to Cease Because Christ Has Redeemed Me from The

Curse of The Law. I Have Eradicated Poverty and Lack, Sickness and Disease, And Spiritual Death in My Life.

I Am a Destroyer of The Works of The Devil. Satan Is Under My Feet. I Have the Victory Through Christ Jesus! I Am Blessed Coming in And Blessed Going Out. I Am Blessed in The City and Blessed in The Field. Everything I Put My Hands to Is Blessed.

I Am the Head and Not the Tail, Above Only and Not Beneath. I Lend to Many Nations, and I Borrow from None.

(Gal. 3, Gen. 22:17-18, Deut. 28, I John 3, Rom. 16, I Corinth. 15, Eph. 1)

WHAT IS OUR ROLE IN GOD'S KINGDOM?

I Enforce God's Authority Here on Earth! Jesus Gave Me the Keys to The Kingdom. With These Keys, I Bind Every Spirit Contrary to The Spirit of God from Manifesting, Operating, Speaking or Coming Against Me. I Believe in And Loose the Immeasurable, Unlimited, And Surpassing Greatness of God's Power in And for Me. This Same Power Resurrected Jesus from The Dead and Seated Him at God's Right Hand–Far Above All Principality, Power, Might, And Dominion and Every Name That Is Named Not Only in This World but In That Which Is to Come. I Have Been Raised with Christ. Christ, Who Is My Life, Has Appeared in Me. Therefore, I Appear with Him in Glory! God Has Girded Me with His Strength and Made My Way Perfect. He Has Brought Me Forth into a L–A–R–G–E, Spacious Place.

God Is My Fortress and My Deliverer. He Has Made Me A Deliverer. I Pursue My Enemies Until I Overtake Them All.

(Luke 10:19, Matt. 28, Matt. 16, Eph. 1, Col. 3, Rom. 6, Psalm 18)

CONSISTENCY OF THE INTERCESSOR

Intercessors should stay consistent in how they pray, in the strategies used, and in the types of prayers they offer up. For example, intercessors should:

1. Pray daily and confess that the Blood of Jesus covers me, my family, and everyone connected to us including all we possess and are concerned with.

2. Keep the covering of the Full Armor of God.

3. Study and confess Psalm 91. Declare that if I dwell in the secret place of the Most High, under His wings, covered with His feathers then no plague can come near me. One thousand may fall at my side and 10,000 at my right hand, but it will not come near me.

    a. No harm will come near me.

    b. No evil will come near me

    c. Angels guard me.

4. Loose angels. We have ministering, protecting, and warrior angels (such as Michael, the archangel).

5. Believe and confess Isaiah 54:17 (KJV) and know that *no weapon, and no tongue can prevail.*

6. Know that Proverbs 16:7 (KJV) tells us that *our enemies can be at peace with us.*

7. Pray against all persecution (See Mark 10:29), retaliation, and buffeting spirits (II Corinthians 12:7) in Jesus Name. Pray against

all harassing, lying, and tormenting spirits in Jesus' Name (For every situation concerning us and those connected to us).

8. Take full authority over and break the power of the enemy. Reject and cancel in Jesus' name: All curses, evil hope, psychic and soulish prayers, and witchcraft. (That try to come against us and to anyone connected to us).

9. Reject and cancel all words spoken or written against us, our family, and the groups we are connected to. Pray against and resist everything that is contrary to the Word and will of God.

10. Know that God fully protects – Our spirit, soul, and body— socially and financially from anything contrary to the Word and will of God.

11. Always bind every spirit that is contrary to the Spirit of God from manifesting, operating, speaking, or coming against us (our family and groups we are connected to).

12. Cleanse and rid our homes of any spirit contrary to the Spirit of God - This includes any pagan idols, and demonic items. Ask the Holy Spirit to fill our homes with His love, joy, and peace. Call forth and loose ministering angels. Anoint our homes with oil.

13. This should be our position and stance at all Meetings---Before every meeting and gathering, we should have intercession at the beginning of the meeting and pray that individuals would hear beyond our words, and that the eyes of their understanding be enlightened; the hearts would be prepared; pray that God will bring the ones He wants and not satan; We must always use our keys to the Kingdom (binding and loosing—declaring what is legal, illegal, and trespassing).

a. Pray for the restraining power of the Holy Spirit and continue to bind every spirit that is contrary to the Spirit of God from manifesting, operating, speaking, or coming against us.

b. Specifically, bind up spiritual pride, confusion, un-teachable spirit, competition, comparison, envy, jealousy, disruption, interruption, and false prophecy.

c. Bind persecution, retaliation, buffeting spirits, curses, and witchcraft.

d. Bind any robberies, losses, and delays and bind up all hijacking spirits. Proclaim that satan must repay anything and everything stolen (Proverbs 6:31).

e. Loose and call forth truth and conviction. Loose God's will and declare His Kingdom come…loose the blood of Jesus' protection.

14. Loose and call forth the anointing of God, the gifts of the Spirit, love, joy, peace, righteousness. Loose the supernatural favor of God…

a. Ask God to multiply our time, rest, and to provide supernatural strength and stamina. Pray for the mind of Christ (Wisdom, knowledge, understanding, discernment, revelation, interpretation).

b. Pray (Deut. 28) – Everything that we touch with our hands will be blessed.

c. Pray Proverbs 16:3 (NKJV) *"Commit your works to the Lord, and your thoughts will be established."*

d. Pray Proverbs 3:6 (NKJV) *"in all your ways acknowledge Him, and he shall direct your paths."*

15. Stand bold, stay equipped, and ready to truly intercede on behalf of others including their cities, state, nation, and world.

Additionally, deeper levels of prayer and intercession should include:

KNOWING THE FULL BENEFITS OF GOD'S CHOSEN FAST

AS WE INTERCEDE FOR OTHERS – ISAIAH 58:6-14 (NIV)

As stated earlier, fasting feeds the spirit man and starves the flesh. The intercessor must maintain the proper balance in the spiritual realm—seeking daily to walk in the spirit by stirring up the Holy Spirit within. In essence, we must always practice the presence of God daily AND ALLOW GOD TO reign in our lives.

God's chosen Fast declares:

- **The Chains of Injustice Have Been Loosed**

- **The Cords of The Yoke Have Been Untied**

- **The Oppressed Have Been Made Free**

- **And Every Yoke Has Been Broken**

- **My Light Has Broken Forth Like the Dawn**

- **Healings Have Quickly Appeared**

- **God's Righteousness Goes Before Me**

- **And The Glory of God Is My Rear Guard.**

- **When I Cry for Help, God Says, Here Am I**

- **My Night Has Become Like the Noonday**

- **The Lord Guides Me Always**

- **He Satisfies My Needs and Strengthens My Frame**

- **I Will Be Called Repairer of Broken Walls (Repairer of the Breach)**

- **Restorer Of Streets with Dwellings.**

- **I Ride on The Heights of The Land**

- **And Feast on The Inheritance of Jacob**

Declaring, Decreeing and Receiving the Inheritance of Jacob for Situations We Encounter.

(See Deuteronomy 32:9, 12-14)

The Lord Alone Leads Me; No Foreign Gods Are with Me. The Lord Feeds and Nourishes Me with The Abundance of The Land and Flock

Continuously study and find other relevant scriptures to engage other areas of warfare you may encounter.

UNDERSTANDING THE ANOINTING

Previously, we discussed the worship experience and practicing the very presence of God in our lives. We spoke about the importance of becoming intimate with God as we build a personal relationship with Him. We mentioned that worship shows our devotion and dependency on God. Worship is what we are committed and devoted to; what we live and would die for and cannot live without; what we love with all our heart, soul, mind, and strength and are willing to sacrifice our entire life for.

We discussed that worship is a spontaneous response to the love that God has for us. During worship, God reveals His glory through us as

He ministers to our hearts. Worship brings heaven down to earth and puts us in a right relationship with the Father. God gives us an Eden experience of peace, love, and joy. (Your Kingdom come—Your will be done in earth as it is in heaven). This occurrence brings about a tangible encounter with God. This encounter reminds us that God is with us and that He is near – we can feel and acknowledge His comfort, His love, His peace, His grace.

All of us can and need to have the presence of God daily in our lives as we fellowship with God. However, after we arise from off our knees and out of our quiet time to face the world---we need to operate with God in our lives. This operation in the Spirit of God is the "anointing" or the "power" of God that is necessary for us to be used and sustained by God. The worship experience is particularly important in understanding the "anointing." The presence of God must first manifest personally in our lives so that His "anointing" or "power" would publicly go into demonstration and operation (with signs, wonders, and miracles following---not defeat).

As we get to know God intimately in worship, we begin to believe in what He can do—in, with, and through us…by the anointing. *When Christ who is our life appears in us…We too appear with Him in Glory* (Colossians 3:4-NKJV). God's Glory includes the weightiness of His presence.

We begin to live, move, and have our being in Him—We walk in the anointing. It cannot be seen but its effects are noticeable like the wind mentioned in John 3:8 (NKJV). The effects of the anointing can be seen with the manifestation of power in our lives. The effect of the anointing will also be seen as prophesied by Isaiah in chapter 11 and as stated by Jesus when the prophecy was fulfilled in Luke 4:18. *The Spirit of the Lord is upon me because He has anointed me…*). The Holy Spirit has seven dimensions as mentioned in Isaiah chapter 11. When we walk in the anointing, we will receive all these dimensions in our everyday lives…this means that we have the boldness to walk in God's anointing everywhere we go and not just in a church service:

The **Spirit of the Lord** (Eternal God) will rest upon us…as it rested upon Him…This includes the Spirit of:

- **Wisdom** (chokmah in Hebrew) means skillful, wisely, wit, shrewdness,

- **Understanding** (biynah in Hebrew) means perfectly understand,

- **Counsel** (etsah in Hebrew) means plan, prudence, purpose,

- **Might** (gbuwrah in Hebrew) **means force, valor, victory, mastery, mighty act, power, strength,**

- **Knowledge** (da/ath in Hebrew) means cunning, aware, wittingly,

- **Fear of the Lord.** (yir'ah in Hebrew) **means reverence of God.**

When we experience God's presence, He brings us into a state of wholeness and a oneness with Himself. This is the place where He is ready to use us. When God begins to use us, we need the anointing which is the daily power to fight off our carnal life, our flesh, demons, sickness, the powers of hell and darkness and everything that is contrary to the Spirit of God. Without the anointing, there will be no growth, victory, or blessing in our walk with Christ.

The anointing comes with power and boldness and not fear. The anointing mentioned in Isaiah 10:27 comes from the Hebrew word (Shemen 8081) which means: to grow fat; richness that is only released by pressing or crushing (as the oil released from the olive). (When we are sick and tired of being where we are—we either die in that state or we are forced to go higher and grow. We must allow the oil to be released from the pressing and crushing that may occur in our life). Life with God should reflect continual growth that is described as line upon line and precept upon precept—here a little and there a little (See Isaiah 28:9-10). The oil is then separated from the rest of the fruit. The anointing is the increase of the power of God within us. This is the fullness of God being manifested and the separation of functioning in our carnal flesh (of pride, arrogance, reoccurring sin etc..) to functioning through the "Spirit of God" within our lives. Walking in this anointing will break and destroy the yoke of the enemy who tries to come into our lives.

Anointing mentioned in I John 2:27 is the Greek word Chrisma (5545) that comes from 5548 Chrio (the Anointed One). Here anointed means endowment of the Holy Spirit; separating us to God. The gift of the Holy Spirit is what brings us into all truth. (God poured out His gift--the Spirit of Truth in Acts 2 as prophesied by the Prophet Joel). God poured out of His Spirit...not just to fellowship with us in worship...but so that we could partake in His Divine nature...No longer living carnally but in the supernatural. When the super becomes "natural," we are able to walk as God's witnesses in the earth! AMEN—so be it Lord.

In the anointing Deep calls Deep...in *Psalm 42:7 (KJV) David says: Deep calleth Deep at the noise of thy waterspouts. All thy waves and billows are gone over me.* David was so engulfed in the power of God that His Spirit was in continuous fellowship with God...He communicated with God with His spirit. There is a place in God...where there is absolute silence, no words, and no or little movements. When we come to this place in the deep, we allow the waves of the anointing to sweep over us. As Deep calls Deep...our spirit must join with the Spirit of God...to receive the anointing of God. This experience requires a daily death...dying to pride and arrogance, dying to sin ... living in humility, obedience, and in a state of seeking after the deep. It also requires flowing in the spirit of unity as we function in the body of Christ.

The anointing allows us to walk in and inherit the very Kingdom of God here on earth as we take our stand against the wiles of the devil. We wrestle not against flesh and blood (therefore, flesh and blood weapons cannot help us and will not work), but against principalities, against powers, against the rulers of the darkness of this age, against spiritual hosts of wickedness in the heavenly places (See Ephesians 6:11-12). Therefore we must fight at an elevated level (in the anointing) to destroy spiritual wickedness in high places (spiritually, we must punch high and never low). We must BREAK AND DESTROY THE YOKES…OF WICKEDNESS such as the master demon "belial".

> *Isaiah 10:27 (b) "and the yoke shall be destroyed because of the anointing." (KJV)*

> *Read I John 2:18-27. Verse 27 states: "but the anointing which you have received from Him abides in you, and you do not need that anyone teach you; but as the same anointing teaches you concerning all things, and is true, and is not a lie, and just as it has taught you, you will abide in Him." (NKJV)*

BREAKING AND DESTROYING THE DEMONIC INFLUENCE OF bELIAL

(THE MASTER DEMON OF WICKEDNESS)

In the New Testament the word belial (in the Greek) means – worthless. Belial is an epithet (descriptive name or a title—adjective, noun) of satan.

> *2 Corinthians 6:15 (Amplified Bible) states…." What harmony can there be between Christ and belial (the devil). Or what has a believer with in common with an unbeliever." The KJV states: And what concord hath Christ with Belial? Or what part hath he that believeth with an infidel?*

Belial's job is to keep us living under the curse (Poverty & lack; Sickness & disease; and Spiritual Death) that Christ redeemed us from. He is the yoke that tries to bind us and hinder us from moving forward. The children of belial are under his control. *I Timothy 4:1-2 (KJV) state: "Now the Spirit speaketh expressively that in the latter times some shall depart from the faith, giving heed to seducing spirits, and doctrines of devils; speaking lies in hypocrisy; having their conscience seared with a hot iron."*

THIS IS THE WORK OF bELIAL AND HIS CHILDREN THAT LEADS OTHERS ASTRAY.

In the Old Testament the word B'liyaal (Hebrew in the Strong's—1100) means without profit, worthlessness, destruction, wickedness, evil naughty, ungodly. It comes from another Hebrew word 1097 that means failure, to fail, wear out, decay, nothing.

Deuteronomy 13:13 (KJV) states: "Certain men, children of belial, are gone out from among you and have withdrawn the inhabitants of their city, saying, let us go and serve other gods which you have not known."

Judges 19:1-29 (KJV) give one of the most perverted stories I have ever read in the Bible…caused by belial and his children. This is the story of the Levite's concubine who died after being repeatedly raped and abused all night long. Verse 22 tells us that these were sons of belial. (This is a sign of a seared conscience). Let us learn from this story and refuse to become distraught by belial in our lives.

To be led by the Spirit, we must always understand the Spiritual realm. Galatians 5:18 says: *If you are led by the Spirit, you are not under the law. Christ has redeemed us from the curse of the law.* However, we must fight to advance, maintain, and occupy God's Kingdom that is rightfully ours. Valiant men must take it by force.

WE MUST LOOSE OURSELVES AND OTHERS FROM THE CURSE OF bELIAL TO MOVE FORWARD WITH GOD.

- When individuals feel worthless…we must bind up and rebuke belial

- If there is overwhelming wickedness trying to overtake a situation…bind up and rebuke belial.

- When people feel tired, exhausted with life, and useless…bind up and rebuke belial.

- When failure seem to lurk…bind up and rebuke belial

- When there is backsliding and a constant feeling of returning to a sinful life…bind up and rebuke belial.

- When you constantly hear that your life will amount to nothing…bind up and rebuke belial.

- When there is much perversion…bind up and rebuke belial. Ask God to deliver you from this situation.

- When we identify that there is a sense of a seared conscience—individuals who just do not care, we are to intercede for deliverance from belial…bind him up, rebuke him and cast him out in the name of Jesus. As we pray for others, we can expect God to bring deliverance.

DAYS OF ELIJAH AND TODAY!

As intercessors, let us desire for the power and might of the true God to rain down on us. During the days of Elijah, there was a direct confrontation of false gods and the true and living God. The false gods of the day appeared strong and overpowering. But we all know that our God, the true God, never changes. *He is the same God of yesterday, today, and forever (Hebrews 13:8).* Our God is Omnipotent (all powerful), Omniscient (all knowing); and omnipresent (He is everywhere). *I John 4:4 (NKJV) tells us "…He who is in you is greater than he who is in the world."* Therefore, we can be confident that the power of the true God will always be with us as He works signs, wonders, and miracles amid evil.

During the days of Elijah, an evil King Ahab allowed his wife Jezebel to bring in false prophets to kill and destroy the true prophets of God. The true prophet Elijah became nervous and afraid when he thought that he was the only godly prophet left. I believe that the spirit of belial was trying to overtake Elijah and caused him to feel insignificant and worn out. However, God told Elijah in I Kings 19:18 that He preserved 7000 just like him who did not follow the false gods. Elijah had to press through his concerns and mindset to hear the voice of God. One of belial's strategy is to cause fear or concern to overwhelm us amid evil. However, we are to remember that God has a remnant – a true people that He has preserved. For example:

In 2 Samuel 3:1, David and others fought off Saul's religious control and converted the Kingdom back to God.

Acts 1 and 2 tell us how God used 120 people who stayed in one place with unity until the power of God came to change the world. Today, we are still benefiting from this commitment by believers of the faith.

God is requiring a deeper level of passion and adoration from us in the wake of evil so that His anointing will increase to break and destroy every evil force. We must take God's anointing into every area of intercession as we pray for our family, cities, state, nations, and the world.

We must remember, however, that we cannot encounter the anointing and then try to go back and live any way we want to in the sinful flesh. If we do so, the devil will have a field day in our lives. However, if we are earnest in our walk with God, He will take us to deeper levels and higher heights. God moves in the storms and earthquakes as well as in the still quiet winds—He has many moods—but His desire is for us to live in the anointing.

Today, God's Kingdom has come, and Jesus declared that one of the signs of the manifested Kingdom of God is that these signs shall follow them that believe; in my name shall they cast out devils (Mark 16:17). **Intercessors, be bold and do not back down. After you are delivered, then God has called you to deliver others through your prayers and intercessions. Allow your Effectual Fervent prayers to avail much!**

SUMMARY, REVIEW, AND PERSONAL REFLECTIONS

1. In your own words, what does James 5:16 say about effectual fervent prayer?

2. What is *intercession*, and why do we intercede?

3. How do we intercede?

4. Describe the 12 strongmen. Can you identify the actions of these strongmen in your life, or in the lives of others?

5. Who are we in God's Kingdom?

6. How do we enforce God's Kingdom in the earth?

7. What are some of the benefits of God's Chosen Fast?

8. What is the anointing, and how does God's anointing break and destroy evil?

9. Privately pray and intercede daily. Also, seek opportunities to pray aloud in a corporate setting as you are led to intercede for families, friends, cities, states, nations, and the world. Take Your rightful place as you walk in Kingdom dominion authority. Also, remember to start or join a prayer group which will provide you with opportunities to pray with others in an atmosphere of agreement.

Lastly, I recommend and challenge everyone to read and study the entire Bible annually. Allow God's Word to be the lamp unto your feet and the light unto your pathway. Intercessors, I challenge you to know the Word of God inside out and allow it to become tangible flesh as you boldly and courageously declare Victory in the earth.

NOTES

(This page is intentionally left blank for note taking)

DORN J.B. WALKER is a licensed ordained minister and co-laborer with Christ who ministers the Gospel of God's Kingdom. She attended the Bride of Christ School of Ministry and trained in a ministerial capacity under the leadership of Apostles, Dr. Benjamin Rucker and Dr. Angela Rucker. Walker also attended the Empowerment Theological Institute and Bible Seminary where she received a Doctorate in Divinity.

Since 1987, Dr. Walker has made tremendous contributions to the Body of Christ as a Servant Leader who served in various ministerial, executive, and leadership capacities at several churches in the U.S. Virgin Islands, Washington, D.C., Maryland, and Pensacola, Florida. She currently partners with her husband Apostle John Walker, Jr., the founding pastor of the "Walls of Salvation Church Ministries" in Pensacola, Florida where she serves as an Elder, Prophet, Evangelist, and Vice President and Executive Manager of the nonprofit's daily church operations.

In 1995, Dr. Walker authored her first book *Life After Loss: A Journey into Wholeness* which remained on the publisher's consistent seller list for more than five years. She later authored, *The School of True Worship and Effectual Fervent Prayer* (curriculum book), and the *I AM" Poster and Worship Journal*, and is the artist of the "I AM" (Spoken Word) audio. She has co-authored several ecclesiastical training manuals including the *Outreach Evangelism Manual, Essentials: Your New Life in Christ*, and the *Leadership and Empowerment Training* manuals used to train and equip leaders for over 10 years. She is the founder of the "Oil of Joy Ministry," an outreach to those with broken lives, including prisoners and AIDS patients, and is currently developing the "S.H.E." (Salvations & Healings through Evangelism) Global Movement which provides mentorship and empowerment to women leaders (daughters) called to Ministry.

Dr. Walker is graced with the 5-fold ministry mantles of the Prophet and Evangelist; however, she often flows in the Apostolic. Yet, she stays humble and open to the move of the Holy Spirit and refuses to limit any move of

God in her life. Her unique prophetic evangelism approach to ministry encompasses her call to minister to the complete person—spirit, soul, and body (I Thessalonians 5:23). This ministry includes preaching, evangelism, and street witnessing, ministering at Women's Conferences and conducting wholeness workshops, motivational seminars, and retreats. Dr. Walker publishes the good news of the Gospel, and ministers through praise and worship dances. She is a member of the International Dance Commission of dancing preachers. She was also trained in Dr. Edward Smith's counseling approach to healing from emotional pain.

Dr. Dorn J.B. Walker is a native U.S. Virgin Islander and a graduate of the University of the Virgin Islands where she completed a bachelor's degree in Accounting. Additionally, she completed graduate school course work in Public Administration through the U.S. Department of Agriculture's Graduate School in partnership with the American University in Washington, D.C. She is the wife of Pastor John Walker, Jr., and the mother of three precious children—Tesa, Joshua, and Josiah, son-in-love, Thomas Fabyan, daughter-in-love, Monique Walker, Grand Princess, Azaria, and Grand Prince, Steuart.

Other books and products by Dr. Dorn J.B. Walker can be purchased from www.wallsofsalvation.global. The "I AM" (Spoken Word) is available on all digital platforms.